If You Want a Dog

What Kids Should Know Before Getting a Dog

Spring Taylor

Taking care of a dog is hard work.

You need to train him

come
here

sit

roll
over

jump

and give him many treats.

You need to feed him

and change his water
every day.

You also need to clean him

and groom him.

You need to walk him.

Even on

rainy, sunny, or snowy days.

Don't forget
to pick up after him.

PLEASE
PICK UP
AFTER
YOUR PET

Help him make new friends.

Play together

and have fun.

Read to him

until he falls asleep.

Dogs are not perfect

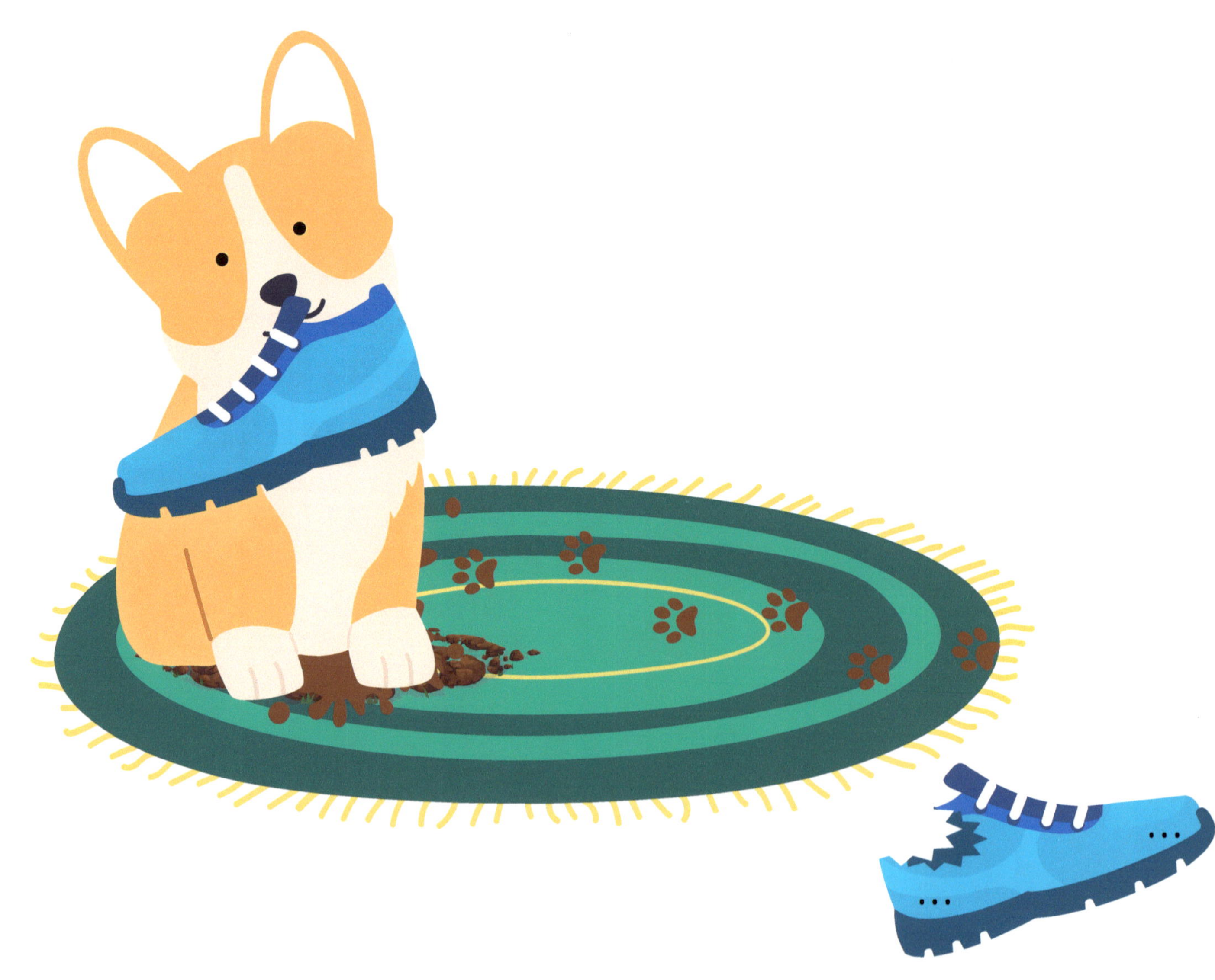

but they are full of love.

If you can do all this,
you are ready.

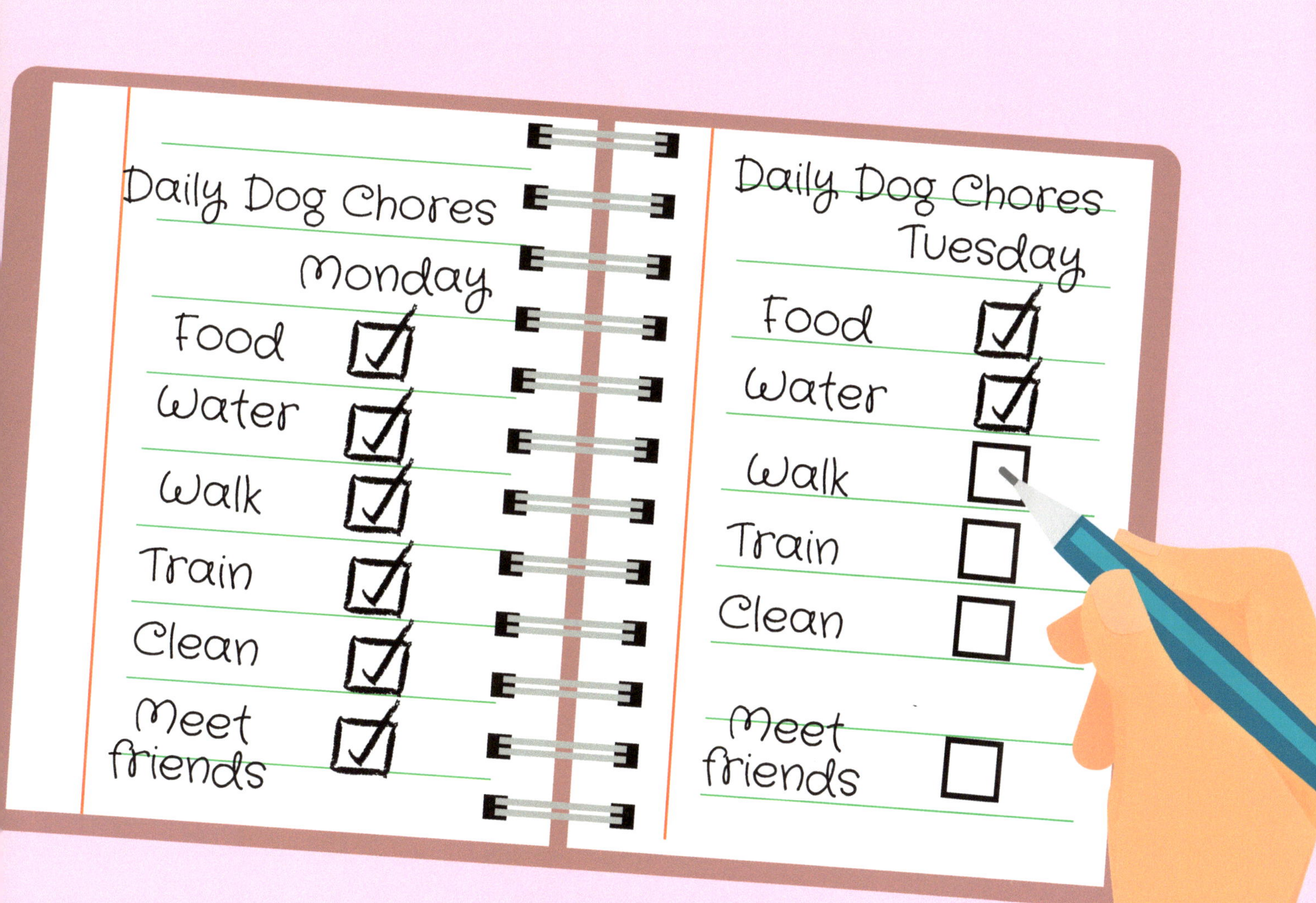

Ready for
a beautiful friendship.